1 MONTH OF
FREE
READING

at
www.ForgottenBooks.com

By purchasing this book you are eligible for one month membership to ForgottenBooks.com, giving you unlimited access to our entire collection of over 1,000,000 titles via our web site and mobile apps.

To claim your free month visit:
www.forgottenbooks.com/free907253

ISBN 978-0-266-90326-0
PIBN 10907253

For support please visit www.forgottenbooks.com

Historic, Archive Document

Do not assume content reflects current scientifi
knowledge, policies, or practices

Sout   e

INDEX.

What Do You Want?

Should we write a catalogue and fill it with our statements all the way through, then the reader would have to accept us or reject us. We disapprove of everything being on one side. If a tree bears all its fruit on one side it will break. So we will not do all the writing in this catalogue. Our catalogue contains straight facts of merit of special fruits, not exaggerated statements of novelties and new fruits. Our customers help us write our catalogue. How? We write to them and ask what they want information on, and what fruits do well with them, and what fruits don't do well with them, and what varities we should discard from our catalogue as being worthless. Come and join us and we will make your experience be exactly *what our customers say* of our dealings with them. Please allow us to introduce to you our agent, *Merit.* He will win in the long run and you will be pleased. This book does his talking, and a one cent postage stamp is his whole expense, (the purchasers always pay agents traveling expenses.)

We will give you orchard reports and letters telling of our dealings directly with farmers and fruit growers. Some of them of your county. Take their word, they have tried us, we want your complete order. If you have any doubt of our square dealings, then we want only a trial order. In either case, let us make acquaintance *this year.* If you desire to experiment,—buy a long list of different fruits, fertilize, nurse, prune and wish for trees to luxuriate that were not suited to your section, then this catalogue is not for you. But if you wish a catalogue containing varieties that have stood the test and have proven to be the MOST PROFITABLE for commercial orchards, then this catalogue is for you.

Our main object is to supply trees directly to customers for commercial orchards, principally in the south half of the Gulf Coast States.

OUR MOTTO.—Honesty is the best policy. Merit will win in the long run.

REFERENCES:

Bank of Thomasville..................................Thomasville, Ga.
R. W. Glading......................................Thomasville, Ga.
J. L. Lee, Postmaster..............................Thomasville, Ga.
Prof. B. Irby.......................................Raleigh, N. C.
Dr. H. E. McKay, Pres. Miss. State Hort. Society..Madison Station, Miss.
Citizens Banking and Trust Co......................Thomasville, Ga.
And our customers everywhere.

GUIDE TO THE CULTURE

——OF——

Pears, Plums and Other Fruits, Giving the Latest Information Known.

Thomasville, the home and the headquarters of the LeConte, has all the old trees, except the original tree, and one of these old trees, now twenty-four years old, is the picture of health and beauty. It's largest yield was sixty bushels marketed besides the culls. We have a photo of this tree. It measures 43 feet across its boughs and 17 inches in diameter at the trunk, the largest pear tree in South Georgia. The above is given simply to show what they can do.

THE LECONTE PEAR—ITS HISTORY.

The original LeConte pear tree was bought in 1850, under the name of Chinese Sand Pear, from some nurseryman in Philadelphia, by John LeConte, of that city, and presented to his niece, Mrs. J. M. B. Harden, of Liberty county, where it was planted. The tree is now vigorous and healthy, has never blighted nor been injured by any disease, and is a regular annual bearer. As much as forty bushels of fruit has been gathered from the tree in a season. In 1869 cuttings were taken from this tree to Thomas county, Georgia, and planted, a few of which grew and are now twenty-five years old, and owned by Mr. L. L. Varnedoe. These trees are in a perfectly healthy condition and of a size that would surprise any one having no knowledge of the luxuriant growth of the LeConte.

PETER KIEFFER'S CELEBRATED PEAR.

The Sand Pear of Japan, so far as relates to the older trees growing in this section of America, if not in other parts, he certainly introduced. Numerous trees were fruiting here between thirty and forty years ago. The fruit is regarded as of little culinary value, but much esteemed for its delightful perfume. Mr. Kieffer raised seedlings from his tree which were sold yearly from his little nursery. He grew close to the Bartlett (your Williams' Bon Chretien), and the branches of the two interlaced. Some slight difference in seedling was noticed, and it was preserved for sale. This provoked what is, from the above facts, reasonably believed to be a true cross, the Kieffer pear. The fine red cheek, and some general appearance to the Flemish Beauty, has caused the statement to appear in our pomological works that it is a cross with the Flemish Beauty. Mr. Kieffer grafted and sold a few here and there for five dollars each; but though he distributed among his few horticultural friends annually fruit that would make the most cold-souled epicure leap with joy, no effort was made by any one to place it properly on the market. At length the great Centennial Exposition came. Mr. Kieffer had some on exhibition; these excelled in size, beauty, flavor—everything, indeed, for which any pear could possibly be esteemed. The original Kieffer pear tree is still standing in Mr. Kieffer's grounds.

PEARS FOR PROFIT.

But little investigation is required in order to learn that a pear that will sell well is not necessarily a pear of fine eating qualities. The best market fruit is the one which presents the best appearance on the market. Those who have eaten the Bartlett can testify as to its good eating qualities, but the following from P. M. Kiely's Fruit and Vegetable Guide, will be a surprise to the staunch friends of the Bartlett and will be encouraging to the fortunate growers of the LeConte: "One day we had twenty barrels of fine LeContes, and side by side with them were offered twenty barrels of good Bartletts from a Missouri grove. To our surprise the LeContes brought fifty cents more per barrel than the reigning favorite."

The flavor of the LeConte is of variable quality, being classed by some as excellent. The flavor of the Kieffer ranges wider than that of the LeConte—from best to worst—according to taste and condition of fruit when eaten. Let the flavor of the two pears be what it may, it is nevertheless a settled fact that they are sure and fast selling profitable pears. The introducer of the LeConte to the county, Mr. Varnedoe, four years ago gathered six hundred barrels for shipping, besides culls, from an orchard of three hundred trees. The three hundred trees occupy six acres. This was one hundred barrels per acre. The above is no speculation as to what could be done, but was actual count of the barrels after the heads were put in.

While such a large yield cannot be expected every year, still it shows very clearly that there is good money to be made in growing pears. The proper thing to be done, and just what all of the thoughtful and conservative farmers of the Gulf Coast States are doing, is to plant o few acres in pears and other fruits, and yearly plant till they are owners of a fine orchard.

PEAR SHIPMENTS JULY 15, '94.

Pears have been moving lively duiing the past week, something like twelve hundred barrels having been shipped, besides a large quantity in crates. Very nearly two thousand barrels have been shipped this season. It was thought at one time that the crop would be a total failure, but this doesn't look much like it. Prices have been better this season and have held up better than ever before. They have ranged all the way from five to seven dollars per barrel. The average price in the Northern market yesterday was $5.50. This will net about $4.25, which makes the business a very profitable one. A large per cent of the crop is to be shipped yet and it is hoped that prices will hold up the balance of the season.—Times-Enterprise.

ORCHARD REPORTS—LECONTE PEARS.

This summer one grower here with an orchard of 5 acres, 250 trees, barrelled 180 barrels, and received on an average net, $4.50 per barrel, or the net sum of $162 per acre. He is now shipping a large crop of Kieffers.

Another grower here, the best yield we had this season, showed me the checks net of $145.41 for LeConte pears off of his pet ¼ of an acre. Can prove the above or give 1,000 trees if we fail.

Still another grower, who has a large orchard, on being asked how much did his trees yield per annum said, some years a great deal more than others, but on an average the trees netted him 50 cts. each. Fifty trees to the acre gives him $25. How does that compare with your farm crops?

ORCHARD REPORTS—KIEFFER PEARS.

"We are in receipt of a box of fine Kieffer pears from Mr. H. M. S., of Texas. They are superb in size and beauty and have as fine quality as that pear is capable of having. Mr. S. is the champion of Kieffer and Le-Conte on LeConte stock and his results speak louder than words: On LeConte roots he gets seven bushels of Kieffer pears to the tree, while on **French stock** he got seven hundred bushels from two hundred trees. One half as productive. It does one's heart good to see Mr. S's healthy and vigorous LeConte orchard on their own roots. I must say they form massive walls of luxuriating beauty and symmetry that is not equaled by any orchard I have seen elsewhere."—Southern Horticultural Journal.

The following is a table showing the net proceeds from one and a half acres for five years:

1886..$ 623.12
1887.. 221.10
1888.. 565.20
1889.. 808.57
1890.. 317.79

          Total...$2,535.78

This shows an average of $507.15, or $338.10 per acre, each year. Very good income, but nothing like the possibilities of that fruit. I have gathered as many as fifteen bushels from one tree. The trees are now greener, more healthy, growing more rapidly than I ever saw them, and are full of fruit buds for next crop. Very few have died this year and that only on bad lands, where cotton has always died with root rot. I have not manured much nor cultivated after the trees were three years old.

I have not lost any fruit this year nor any money in my sales, having confined my shipments to my old reliable, prompt and clever commission men.   Respectfully,

Grimes county, Texas.   R. D. BLACKSHEAR.

LOCALITIES AND SOILS.

The locality which is best suited to the LeConte is the belt of country lying between the apple and citrus belts, or practically the Gulf Coast States. The most successful commercial orchards are within 150 miles of the Atlantic and Gulf Coasts. The Kieffer practically has an unlimited territory. It thrives well both North and South.

As to the soil: While the LeConte and Kieffer will live and bear fruit on any soil, still it will not be profitable as a commercial fruit on any but drained soil. The better land is for corn and cotton the better it is for pears.

An orchard that is expected to bear fruit for twenty or more years, must have a strong subsoil, and if it has not enough top soil, then one must be made by planting renovating crops and plowing them under. Rye for a winter crop, and clover, peas, beggar weeds, and weeds for summer crops. Some horticultural writer once wrote. "never plant a pear tree over a tile drain." This was written to impress forcibly the great importance of well drained land for pear trees. For the **most successful** commercial orchard the land must be **well** drained, or made so by drainage; must have a fertile soil with a strong clay subsoil from four to six inches below the top soil.

PREPARATION OF THE SOIL.

Before planting it is best to grow peas, clover or some other renovating crop, turn under while green with a two-horse plow, and ⚫subsoil the ground. Lay off rows and dig holes two feet deep and two feet wide, throw in a little top soil.

PLANTING THE TREES.

Plant trees in prepared hole the same depth it grew in the nursery, except grafted trees, which should be set so the junction will be about three inches under the surface. With a sharp knife cut off every broken and bruised root; letting the cut be on the under side. It is not necessary to use water in planting, but put moist soil next to roots. Have the hole a little higher in the center and place the tree on top of the crown, allowing all the roots to incline downward and not over-lap each other. Fill up the holes so when settled it will be level. Remember the trees grew in firm soil, so be sure and pack the soil as firm as you can, not to bruise the roots. Not so necessary in fall planting, but tight packing is the salvation for spring planted trees.

TIME OF PLANTING.

In this climate, vegetation, although inactive in winter for the formation of leaves and new wood is never so as to new roots. Consequently trees planted in November and December will gain one half a year's growth over trees planted later. By all means plant before March if you can, but plant first of March rather than wait till next fall.

DISTANCES FOR PLANTING.

LeConte...30 by 30 each way
Kieffer...................................... ....25 by 25 "   "
Other Varieties.. ...:................................20 " 20 "   "
Plums, Persimmons and peaches....................20 " 15
Grapes..8 " 10

PRUNING PLUMS AND PEACHES FOR PLANTING.

Remove every branch and cut the top back to the desired height from twenty to thirty inches. When the buds begin to grow rub off all but three to five at the top.

PRUNING PEAR TREES.

The object in pruning is to obtain a low, well balanced tree, with limbs well distributed.

The habit of the LeConte is to send its roots deep into the soil, and its top straight and high in the air. One would not have to witness but once a six foot man standing on a twenty-foot ladder with a fourteen-foot pole in his hand reaching for LeConte pears at the top of the tree to be convinced of the great importance of pruning low. One orchardist here after gathering one crop from some high trees, afterwards cut from eight to ten feet out of the top of his trees, and is pleased with the result.

When the one-year-old trees are planted they should be cut back to eighteen inches or two feet. At two years old they will have branches spreading equally apart around the trunk; three to five of these shoots should be selected to form the main branches on which to build the whole head, and the others should be removed; those reserved should be cut back so when the new shoots come out the tree will spread most which generally leaves the branches only about a foot long. From the shoots produced on these during the season at and below the cut one or two of the strongest are selected on the outer side, and the others rubbed off while they are soft. The trunk must be kept clear of all shoots by rubbing them off as soon as possible. The attention required after this (the second year) will be to maintain a uniform growth among the branches and prevent water-sprouts in the center.

SUMMER PRUNING.

The **proper** time to remove water-sprouts is when the growth first comes to a stand still before they begin to harden and thicken up. If removed at this stage, new sprouts will seldom appear afterwards.

The most **practical,** and probably the best time to remove the sprouts, is when you have the time and a knife.

CULTIVATION AND FERTILIZERS.

The object of cultivation is to produce a large healthy tree. This is accomplished by stirring the soil from three to five inches deep, at least three feet all the way around the tree early in the season, keeping the ground mellow throughout the entire growing period, which if for young trees till about August, and for older trees July 4th. After every rain stir the soil and do not allow a hard crust to form, or the grass to grow.

For a young orchard the first year, frequent cultivation is the best possible fertilizer, afterwards barn yard manure spread around the trees and forked in is the best and cheapest manure. If manure is not convenient, use one pound of cotton seed meal to the tree with a little bone meal added. Most any of our brands of fertilizers will be utilized advantageously by the trees. If the land is fresh, it then contains vegetable mould —nitrogenous material—and the cotton seed is not necessary. Land that will produce one-half a bale of cotton per acre generally will not require fertilizing till the trees begin to bear. Old land that has become heavy and close, caused by the absence of vegetable matter, must have renovating crops grown on it, and *allowed* to *remain*, such as clover, peas, and even grass and weeds. In the fall cut them down so they will rot. In the spring work them in the soil around the trees with commercial fertilizers added. In this way food for the tree is stored in the soil. With the exception of hay and grains, most any crop can be grown between the rows of trees. Truck farming is best; then comes potatoes, cotton. corn, etc., in order named.

A bearing orchard to give best results requires liberal application of potash and phosphoric acid. Two hundred pounds per acre is fair application, but more would be better. But few orchards after they begin to bear require additional nitrogenous fertilizers other than what they derive from the annual vegetable growth.

CULTIVATION FOR BEARING PEAR ORCHARDS.

What is desired is a healthy condition of trees, dark foliage all summer and a crop of large, smooth fruit. The trees are wanted to make a normal healthy growth and no more, say twelve inches of new wood. In some localities with deep rich alluvial soil the above is best accomplished by allowing trees to stand in sod. But, remember, a grass crop and a pear crop is a heavy drain on the soil, and when the trees begin to bear smaller pears, the leaves are smaller and the new growth shorter, then cotton seed hulls ashes and bone dust, or their equals, must be forked in during the spring to produce a full crop and leave the tree vigorous. Most sod orchards should be well broken about every third year to prevent the ground from becoming too compact.

Orchards in many localities where the soil is naturally more compact have to be cultivated annually. Never plow bearing trees till after the fruit is set (till pears are near the size of the end of your little finger.) Then plow with turning plow, and each subsequent plowing should be lighter. Cultivation to cease about July 4. If trees lack vigor fertilize the same as for sod orchard.

CULTIVATION FOR PEACH ORCHARDS.

Each year, in additional to the fertilizers named, the orchard should be sown to rye; or, in situations so far south that it will endure the winter, crimson clover may be sown instead. With the corn, sow rye at the last cultivation. With the potatoes, sow the rye as soon as they are dug, and they should be planted early so as to come off not later than October 1st.

Rye should be sown as soon as the beans are harvested. Of course the rye should each year be plowed under in time to fit the ground for planting the succeeding crop, preferably as soon as it shows heads, putting it far beneath the furrow by using a chain on the plow and plowing as shallow as possible. No crop should be grown in a peach orchard after the third year. The orchard should now have thorough shallow cultivation until the middle of August, at which time it should be sown with rye and oats, half and half and six pecks per acre. The treatment of this fourth year should be repeated each year as long as the orchard is kept, and each year it should be given at least five hundred pounds each of bone dust and muriate of potash per acre. This course will maintain the fertility of the soil, insure strong, vigorous growth during the spring and early summer, furnish abundant food for the growth of pit and kernel, and cause the trees to ripen up fully for winter. Several years ago I sent a drawing to the manufacturers of the Cutaway harrow, after which they made me a harrow having a long beam or spreader so that the sets or gangs of discs could be separated to any distance apart up to eight feet. Of course this would leave a strip in the middle unworked, but its great advantage was that it worked the ground thoroughly close up to the body of the tree while the team did not go close enough to injure the top. The other part could be worked by an ordinary harrow, or after all the orchards had been gone over, the implement could be narrowed up, and the rest cultivated.

Of course, the fruit should be carefully thinned, so as to insure only large perfect peaches. One basket of small peaches will contain as many in number as two baskets of large ones, and as the formation of pit and kernel is what saps the vitality of the trees, small peaches draw as severely on the trees as the same number of large ones, and one basket of the larger will sell for more money than two or three of the smaller.

MARKETING PEARS.

1st. Ship hand picked, sound fruit; no drops. If too fully matured, don't ship; they will rot.

2nd. Separate the primes from the inferior; pack in separate packages and mark each grade No. 1 and 2.

3rd. Pack tightly and solidly to prevent rolling around, rolling bruises and rots them.

4th. The appearance is improved if each pear is wrapped in paper; it keeps them bright and prevents bruising, and scarifying, still this is not absolutely necessary.

5th. Avoid rough, heavy crates with unplaned wood; they should be smooth and well ventilated.

6th. To pack in barrel, make a nice close layer in the bottom of barrel by placing blossom end or sides of pears next to bottom of average pears, fill in the barrel gently, shaking several times. Fill so as to get it as even on top as possible, and about two inches above top of barrel. With a good press, shove the head down to its regular place, then nail securely. They should be tight enough to mash the top layer, but when you do that it will save the barrel.

7th.   Ventilate barrels by cutting holes on top, bottom and sides.

TO A LITTLE STALK OF COTTON.

Little puny stalk of cotton,
　　You've just beheld the light of day;
If we could but know your future
　　Or your destiny portray,
We might have some satisfaction
　　And could work with better pluck,
But alas ! we'll have to trust you,
　　Yes, trust God and you and luck.

In the past you have deceived us
　　That is for the past few years;
You have caused us many heart-aches,
　　You have caused us many fears,
Now you'll surely have to hustle,
　　To regain lost confidence,
For you know you're lots of trouble
　　And a terrible expense.

Soon you'll grow and thrive and flourish,
　　And begin to look so well,
'Till we farmers will have courage
　　And more goods to "niggers" sell.
But we aint'er going ter trust you
　　Like we trusted you last year,
For now we've got some s'perience
　　That cost us mighty dear.

We've got you rated mighty low,
　　Your credit's gone to smash,
For you have ceased to bring us in
　　That mighty stuff called—cash.
One half bale to the acre,
　　Is all that we can "figger" on,
At six cents, it will take it all
　　To feed the "nigger" on.—Ex.

THE NEW SOUTH.

The cotton farmers of the South are at last realizing the fact that there is no money in cotton, so little returns for their efforts. Now as you are going to make a change and raise something that there is more money in than in cotton, let me ask your attention to the inducements offered by fruit growing and other horticultural pursuits. Study the possibilities of the Pear, Plum, Peach, Persimmon, Grape and other fruits. Take advantage of unequaled climate, fertile and responding soil. Consider the great facilities of the railroad in placing a market in a few hours run of your orchard. Ask the farmers ot Amite City, La., Crystal Springs, Miss., Fort Valley, Ga., and of other fruit centers how was it that they removed mortgages, paid old debts, improved their places and homes, and ask why their lands have enhanced in value. Don't ask them how much cotton they plant. A thorough study of the above subjects will reveal to you the fact that you are in the grandest country in America and that profitable fields are only awaiting your plow, pruning shears and fruit wagon. When you take advantage of the opportunities offered by your country, then you will realize that you are living in the deserving and true New South.

ORANGE COUNTY, FLA., July 27th, 1893.

B. W. Stone & Co.,
The trees were better than catalogued. They were perfectly satisfactory. Well pleased with **no agents.** Your dealings will secure my future orders. Yours respectfully,
F. D. STAPLEFORD.

PUTNAM COUNTY, FLA., July 24th, 1893.

B. W. Stone & Co.,
GENTLEMEN: I take pleasure in stating that the trees I bought of you came in nice condition and were fully as represented, they have made fine growth, I have **lost none.** I will send you a respectable order soon. I only wish that all nurserymen would deal as squarely as you do.
Very respectfully,
LOUIS FALK.

LECONTES IN TEXAS.

ALVIN, BRAZORIA CO., TEX., Aug. 20, '94.—The LeConte pear crop is harvested and sold and the net yield has been $2 per bushel. The Alvin country has demonstrated the fact that the pear is a success, for nowhere are they exceeded in size, flavor or beauty. The largest LeConte weighed eighteen ounces; grown by Col. Miller on his Fairyland orchard, and he had sixteen that aggregated 11½ pounds. One bushel shipped to St. Louis brought an order for 100 bushels. General satisfaction was expressed. The Kieffer trees are full to breaking down and many bushels have had to be gathered to save the trees.—Galveston News.

SEASON 1894-95.

INTRODUCTION.

In presenting herewith our annual price list of Pear, Plum, Peach and other fruit trees, we would say to our old customers that we expect to maintain our reputation, and to our prospective customers we would say, give us a trial order and we will convince you that our trees are unequalled in every particular. Give headquarters a trial and quit agents.

ANNOUNCEMENT.

The proprietors wish to state that it gives them pleasure to be able to offer to their customers the nicest lot of trees that has yet been grown, and that increased patronage has enabled us to enlarge our business, and therefore we are better equipped to handle our large lot of trees. Thanking our customers for their past favors. we call their attention to our circular and prices.

WRITE US.

When you receive your trees we want you to write us. When the trees grow we want you to write us. When the trees bear we want you to write us. If any disease or insect appears we want you to write us, so we can aid you. We take all of the leading agricultural and horticultural papers and keep abreast with progressive horticulture. We study horticulture, we delight in horticultural works and love to correspond with our customers on horticultural subjects.

NATURAL ADVANTAGES.

The natural advantages of our soil, climate and location give us facilities for supplying trees of the finest quality at the lowest prices. Hence the secret by which we give our customers **entire** satisfaction.

TRAVIS COUNTY, TEXAS, July 24th, 1892.

B. W. Stoue & Co,

GENTLEMEN: The trees you sent me last winter came in good time and excellent condition. I can now account for the reason you sell so cheap; you have **no agents** and sell for **spot cash.**

Yours truly,

J. H. COLLETT.

NO AGENTS.

We employ no regular agents. We want each planter to be his own agent and order direct from HEADQUARTERS and pay **first** cost and **no** other—then he will not be deceived and we will not be misrepresented.

Have you bought trees of agents? Did you pay high prices and then get deceived? Could you find agents afterwards to get him to make trees good? Now we EARNESTLY ask you to give us a trial. We sell at about one-half the agent's prices. **We support no middle man.** We guarantee our trees to be true to name, and you can find us, for *we* have a regular place of business. and have a reputation to maintain.

Houston, Co., Tex., July 31, '94.
Messrs. B. W. Stone & Co.,
Thomasville, Ga.
Gentlemen: We are pleased with your system as the cost of the agent is left in the **purchasers pocket.** These trees are growing fine and vigorous without the loss of one. The extra trees at the ordinary price nearly pays the freight.
Yours truly,
A. J. C. DUNNAM.

Waller, Co., Tex., Aug. 1, '94·
B. W. Stone & Co.,
Thomasville, Ga.
Dear Sir: You were prompt. The packing was good, and the counting above the number of trees ordered.

I like the system you use, for then the **agent's profits** do not have to be paid by the purchasers.

If you will send me six or eight catalogues when they are out I shall take pleasure in handing them to those that I think likely to buy trees. Yours truly,
J. C. PETTY.

Frio, Co., Tex., Aug. 3, '94.
B. W. Stone & Co.,
Thomasville, Ga.
The trees ordered last fall came promptly and in perfect order. The counting, the quality, the packing, etc., were such as would please any reasonable man. Your plan having *no agents saves* many a hard earned *dollar* for the purchaser. I greatly prefer Southern to Northern grown stock. Respectfully,
Z. C. ROWLAND.

Washington, Co., Tex., Aug. 3, '94.
B. W. Stone & Co.,
Thomasville, Ga.
I am much pleased with your method of dealing *without agents.* Two or three weeks befo.e I sent

you my order, I gave an order to an agent of a company who charged me from 25 cents to one dollar per tree, embracing same sorts you sent me for 10 cents each, with 2 or 3 extra trees; and then you shipped so promptly that I had them set out long before I received those from the agent. Your plan of dealing without agents is certainly a great saving to purchasers.
Respectfully,
T. W. MORRIS.

Claiborne, Co., Miss., Aug. 13, '94.
Messrs. B. W. Stone & Co.,
Thomasville, Ga.
Dear Sirs: Your system, no agents, is the best for the *purchaser*, at least, for the same trees bought of agents would have cost me about three times as much as was paid for them, an average of only about 8 cents apiece.

Your promptness and packing can not be complained of, and as to your *counting* your errors in *my* case were all in buyer's favor, having sent me more trees than were ordered.
Yours respectfully,
B. H. MAGRUDER.

Abita Springs, La., Aug. 3, '94.
Messrs. B. W. Stone & Co.,
Thomasville, Ga.
Gentlemen: Trees a complete success, due specially to the well packed prompt arrival and good quality of the trees, having lost none. I thank you *also* for your *liberal way to count.*

Your system of no agent is the best, as many of my neighbors have complained often of having been fooled by agents, asking high prices for very poor and untrue stock. Believe me.
Yours truly,
E. COGIN.

NO CHARGES.

We make no charges for packing or drayage.

TERMS.

Cash with order. "Owe no man anything" *that we remain friends.*

C. O. D. Parties who prefer to pay on delivery of the goods can avail themselves of that privilege by sending one-half cash with the order, and paying the balance collect on delivery; the charges for collecting and returning money to be paid by purchaser.

REMITTANCES.

By P. O. or Express Money Order, Registered Letter or New York Exchange.

Do not send private check.

FREIGHT OR EXPRESS.

Always state whether you wish trees forwarded by freight or express. If by freight be sure and order in time to let us procure through rates for you. It is much cheaper. Do not order trees shipped to a flag station unless you have arranged with us to prepay freight.

NOT NECESSARY.

To prepay freight or express charges, except to flag stations.

SHIPPING SEASON.

We commence shipping so soon as the trees ripen up their wood, which is the last of October, and continue till about the first of March. It is best to order early so you can be sure and get exactly what you want.

PRUNING BEFORE SHIPPING.

It would save about twenty-five per cent. on freight and express charges if purchasers would have trees pruned before shipping.

JAPAN PERSIMMON.

The persimmon is rather tender and late spring frosts are its greatest drawback.

The fruit resembles in appearance a large smooth tomato, and its flavor is excellent. The tree bears very early (second year) and is very productive. One tree five years old, nine feet high, had on it October 1st, two hundred and five matured specimens. Our trees are all worked on hardy native roots.

They should be cultivated very little after fruit sets, as much cultivation causes fruit to drop prematurely.

JAPAN PLUMS.

Japan Plums are one of the most promising fruits for southern fruit culture. The fruit is mostly large, flesh firm, and of excellent quality, and with small pit. The fruit keeps and ships well, and would make good canned fruit but their quality has so far prevented them from reaching the can.

Of about 30 different varieties of the Japan Plum, we have selected only the most satisfactory and promising. Our list gives a succession from the earliest to the latest. They are fine keepers and can be shipped to any part of the United States. Have been shipped to Paris and remained in good condition nine days after arrival. This season we kept one on our mantle twenty-five days after ready to ship.

From the best known and most promising varieties of Japan Plums we select those that are destined by all known facts to prove the most profitable commercially.

THE MARIANNA PLUM.

The Marianna is the finest and most popular stock for plums. It has driven other varieties out of the field for the following reasons:

The Chicasaw plums, also peaches, will sprout, and in a short time the sprouts will become an eternal nuisance by sapping the tree and by being constantly on hand.

Says Mr. Munson, of Texas: "I know nothing better nor nothing so good as the Marianna for stock."

Plums propagated on peach or peaches propagated on plum will not live long unless the trees are grafted low and when planted in orchard are set low so the trees will put out roots of their own. We propagate all of our peaches on peach, plums on plum and pears on pear so as to give the orchardist no trouble.

HATANKIO. Variable in shape, good size, smooth, bright yellow skin and flesh, juicy, sub-acid, cling. Earliest to bear, was ready to ship June first, is very prolific and the season with color and size makes it a very profitable fruit.

BERCKMANS. (True Sweet Botan.) Much like the Abundance. A more straggling grower. Ripens just ahead of it.

ABUNDANCE. (Yellow Fleshed Botan.) Medium in size, varying from nearly spherical to distinctly sharp-pointed. Ground color, rich yellow overlaid on sunny side with dots and splashes of red and sometimes nearly red. Flesh deep yellow, juicy and sweet, of good quality, cling. A strong upright grower has a tendency to overbear. Ripens about June 10 here which also is at a season to get good prices in the markets.

NORMAND. (Yellow.) Medium to large. Color, clear golden yellow; flesh firm and mealty. Yellow of high quality. Very prolific and ripens after Abundance.

BURBANK. Of the many varieties introduced from Japan, the Burbank is the most promising, its flavor being the best. The tree is universally vigorous with strong limbs. Commences to bear usually at two years of age. The skin is thick and is almost curculio proof, and is an admirable shipping variety. Ripens from 20th to last of June.

BAKER COUNTY, FLA., June 13th, 1893.

B. W. Stone & Co.,

GENTLEMEN: The *Burbank is the best* and most profitable plum we have here. I gathered twenty bushels from one hundred two-year-old trees and they net me from three to seven dollars per bushel.

Yours Respectfully,

W. D. GRIFFING.

SATSUMA. The following is the description given by the introducer, Mr. L. Burbank: "It is earlier than the Kelsey; firm in flesh, much larger, of fine quality, color and form. It is an early and enormous bearer, and the tree grows with more vigor than any other of the Japan Plums I have fruited here. The seed is also the smallest yet seen." Maturity, 1st to middle of July. In many sections the Satsuma is a shy bearer and blooms rather early to depend on it.

BAILEY. Large nearly globular. Ground color, rich orange, overspread with light and bright cherry red, flesh thick and melting, yellow of excellent quality, cling.

KELSEY. This plum is from two to two and a half inches in diameter; flesh a rich yellow with purple cheek. It is a most magnificent plum. It is excellent for canning and drying, and it ships a long distance well. Ripens August and September.

"The Japanese or Kelsey plum, the largest as well as one of the finest varieties of plums offered to the public, has appeared almost daily on the market during the past week from Florida. The prices paid as compared with figures paid for the most attractive California plums were very encouraging, and no doubt the Kelsey will be liberally planted throughout the South during the next few years. All the so-called fancy varieties should give way to this new favorite wherever it succeeds."—P. M. Kiely in Fruit Trade Journal.

The objections to the Kelsey are: It often blooms too early and it rots badly in wet seasons, and is a favorite of the Curculio.

The latest to ripen of any Japan Plums yet introduced.

PEARS.

The pears for the Gulf Coast region is the Japan strain. We have planted cuttings of hardy Japan pear trees, and they are so very hardy and vigorous that we use them as well as LeContes to graft the Kieffer Garber and others on.

All pears offered are grown on thrifty LeConte and Japan stocks.

LECONTES FROM CUTTINGS.

Our LeContes are all guaranteed to be pedigree trees; that is trees that have never been contaminated with the sap of French or Quince stock. It is a thrifty tree, heavy bearer, fruit of variable quality, very large and showy, a good shipper, and so far has been the most profitable pear grown. The LeConte pear crop this year was damaged by the spring freeze, but sales have been large and the prices good, barrels netting $4 to $7. Ripen in July. Our trees are graded carefully into three sizes.

KIEFFER.

The Kieffer, with its thrift, hardiness, beauty, early bearing qualities, size of fruit, with excellent keeping and shipping qualities, has become the pear for profit. The fruit ripens in September and October and can be kept in a cool place till December. It comes in at a season when other fruit is scarce, and the large yellow pears with small black dots command their own prices. Trees bear four years after setting, and no tree bears more abundantly unless it is the LeConte. Every year it gains favor. It is hardy, it is beautiful, and its regular annual abundant yield makes it every where planted the *pear for profit*.

KIEFFERS FROM CUTTINGS.

Kieffer from cuttings are grown just like our LeContes. On their own roots they have fewer roots and are more brittle. but live as well as when grafted and grow with astonishing vigorous growth, They commence to bear earlier, (one or two years sooner) but do not make so large a tree as those grafted. By having a lower tree the fruit will be easily gathered, and about as large crop per acre can be made by planting them closer, say 20 by 20 feet.

GARBER.

This pear is much like the Kieffer in every respect except it bears earlier. It makes the connecting link between the LeConte and Kieffer. The Garber as compared with LeConte is a little later, better flavor, holds up better in shipping. Resists blight much better, blooms out later which enables it to escape more late spring frosts, and like the Kieffer has practically an unlimited area. The Garber does not make as large a tree as the LeConte, hence yields less, but just plant more trees.

THE PEAR CROP MOVING.

Last year Middle and West Florida had a much heavier crop of pears than East Florida, but this year the conditions are reversed. In Baker, Bradford, Alachua, Clay and Duval counties so far as we can learn, the yield will be the heaviest yet harvested. Most of the trees are younger than those in Middle Florida.

"The heavy wind of June 15 started the movement of the crop, a good many windfalls being shipped in the next three days, most of which will not tend to help the market materially. But tne picked crop is now beginning to go forward. The shippers of Middle Florida seem to favor barrels, but in East Florida the 40-pound box is preferred, holding a little over a half bushel. So far the best returns received have been $2 a box gross for LeConte and $3 for Garber's Hybrid. About the only superiority of the latter is its large size.

The orchard of Mr. J. Crawshaw, Jr., of Lawtey, Bradford county, is a fine sight. There are 500 large trees full of fruit, the limbs bending far over with their load, being estimated all the way from five to ten boxes each. There are 1,500 trees in all, the rest being smaller, and estimated at one to three boxes each."—Florida Dispatch.

BARTLETTS.

This pear is quite popular as a market pear, and is one of the best table pears.

IDAHO.

Our experience with the Idaho is that it blights worse than any pear tree we ever saw, hence can not endorse the commendable points we hoped it possessed. To those who wish to further try it we can furnish nice trees.

GRAPES.

In order to be better able to supply our customers, we have selected a few standard varieties of the very best grapes. We have culled the lengthy lists of grapes and offer for sale only a few of the best; such as we can recommend.

CONCORD.—Large, blue-black bunch; quality good; very prolific and vigorous grower. One of the most reliable grapes for general cultivation.

DELAWARE.—Standard of excellence, light red, vine healthy. Unsurpassed for table and white wine.

IVES.—Large and blue, vigorous grower and prolific bearer. Ripens end of June and is a profitable wine grape.

NIAGARA.—Bunch and berry large greenish-yellow. Its fine size and appearance has made it popular. It is vigorous and prolific.

PERKINS.—Large dark-red. It is very valuable, being free from rot, is a fine grower and is very prolific.

SCUPPERNONG.—Absolutely free from all diseases. Muscadine type. Fine for family use and wine.

We can furnish most any variety of grapes that our customers may want. Would be glad to quote you promptly.

PEACHES.

We offer to our customers a few standard varieties of peaches. We have selected such varieties as have been thoroughly tested, and those, taking everything into consideration, that have given the best annual satisfaction.

ALEXANDER (Persian)—Fruit large and early (May).

CRAWFORD'S EARLY (N. Chinese)—Large Yellow (1st of June).

CHINESE FREE (N. Chinese)—Skin white, free stone (1st of July).

GEN. LEE (N. Chinese)—Quality best, Cling stone (1st of July).

ELBERTA (N. Chinese)—Best market peach in Georgia (middle of July).

THURBER (N. Chinese)—Flesh Juicy, free stone (last of July).

ENGLISH WALNUTS.

California Improved soft shell English Walnut. The nut is very large with thin shell. Commences to bear 4 to 5 years.

PECANS.

Texas Large.

MULBERRIES.

Hicks ever bearing.

PRICE LIST.

SEASON 1894-95.

This List Abrogates All Previous Quotations.

	PER 10	PER 100	PER 1000
GRAPES.—			
Delaware, Ives and Niagara..........	$1 25	$9 00	$65 00
Concord and Scuppernongs............	80	6 00	40 00
PEACHES.—			
Alexander, Crawford's Early, Chinese Free, Gen. Lee, Elberta and Thurber...	1 00	9 00	80 00
PEARS.—			
LeContes, one year, 3-4 feet............	60	5 00	40 00
" " " 4-5 "	75	6 50	55 00
" " " 5-7 "	85	7 50	65 00
Kieffer's from cuttings the same price as LeContes.			
Kieffers, one year, 3-4 feet............	90	8 00	70 00
" " " 4-5 "	1 00	9 00	80 00
" " " 5-6 "	1 10	10 00	90 00
" two " branched..........	1 40	13 00	110 00
Garbers, one " 2-4 feet............	1 10	10 00	90 00
" " " 4-6 "	1 30	12 00	100 00
Bartletts, " " 2-4 "	1 40	13 00	
" ". " 4-6 "	1 60	15 00	
Idaho, " " 4-6 "	1 25		
MULBERRIES.—			
One year............................	1 50		
PERSIMMONS.—			
Japan................................	1 40	12 00	
PLUMS.—			
Burbank, Satsuma, Kelsey, Berckmans, Abundance, Normand, Bailey, Hatankio, all on Marianna Plum Stock.			
One year, standard, 4-6 feet............	1 00	9 00	80 00
WALNUTS.—			
English Walnuts, one year old.........	1 60	15 00	
Pecans	80	6 00	

Less than 10 trees at 10 rates. Fifty and 500 trees at 100 and 1,000 rates respectively. Prices given means F. O. B. Thomasville.

REMEMBER.

1st. We guarantee our trees to be true to name, and to ARRIVE in good condition. 2nd. That our trees are not excelled in size, thrift, smoothness and in root power. 3rd. That we take extra care in handling and packing. 4th. That we include some extra trees to help pay freight.

FREE.

MELON SEED.

Read and see what kind. We intend to furnish melon seed for the following reasons:

1st. Beeause our customers often write us for melon seed.

2nd. Because Georgia is recognized all over the U. S. as the home of the melon, and she ships one million melons annually.

3rd. Because we are in the midst of the melon section, hence in a section well adapted to melon seed growing.

4th. Because we can offer genuine seed, and they will be appreciated by melon growers everywhere.

MELON CULTURE.

SOIL.

While melons can be grown on almost any soil, they can not be raised successfully as a field crop unless the soil and location are favorable. The melon will not succeed on heavy clay or lime soils. Light porous sandy loam is the best, and it must be full of humus, or decaying vegetable matter in some form.

The soil should be neither very rich nor very poor—if first would induce a too luxuriant growth of vine and a poorer quality of melons, while the latter would not produce a crop large enough to pay for labor.

Melons follow a good pea crop well. The vines enrich the land and shade it to keep down grass and other obnoxious seeders. An oat patch followed by peas then melons is a good preparation. It is not well to plant melons after grass on account of the seed.

PLOWING.

With a two horse plow turn over your land and completely wrap up all vegetation. Use a chain if necessary on the plow. Do this long enough before planting to allow vegetation plowed under to become well rotted before ready to plant. That will depend on character of vegetation to turn under, but generally about six weeks or two months.

MAKING THE HILLS.

Just before time for planting, mark off across the intended rows with shovel plow ten feet wide. Then with turning plow, two or four furrows, make good deep water furrows ten feet apart for your regular rows across the first marking.

FERTILIZING.

Where it is convenient to do so, make a compost of stable manure, cotton seed meal, phosphate and kainite, not half rotted, but *well* rotted.

If not convenient, use commercial fertilizers as described below.

In the checks up and down the deep furrow, the regular row for two or three feet each way from center, scatter high grade fertilizer at the rates of 200 pounds per acre. Then bed on this with two good furrows. With a hoe or digging fork, work up the hill at checks and make a cross on the hill. Plant one limb of the cross, and every four or five days plant another limb of the cross. The above is practiced when planted before danger of frost is over, otherwise not necessary. Now strow along by the side of the hills, same distances as before, in the two furrows made for bed rows, two hundred pounds each cotton seed meal and phosphate per acre. Then throw two more furrows to cover this.

THINNING THE PLANTS.

When the plants put on four leaves, reduce them to three in the hill. When they get about two feet long, reduce to two in the hill on thin land and to one on rich land.

FURTHER CULTIVATION.

After the plants are up, about once a week throw two more furrows to the bed till the middle is clear. When the plants need work commence with a sweep close to the row and keep just ahead of the vine till they lap in the middle, use the hoe between hills. Do not disturb vines by turning them for cultivation. Remember a little grass or weeds left are not objectionable, for the vines need them to cling to to prevent winds from rolling them over. If any other information is needed we will gladly furnish. We have culled the lengthy list of melons and expect to offer only the gems. We will add to our list as melons of merit prove themselves worthy.

VARIETIES.

GEORGIA'S BEST. (Thomas.)—Oblong in shape, gracefully tapered at each end, color, green with stripes but not near so distinct as the Rattlesnake, meat sweet, crisp but melting. 'Tis strictly a melon for home use and local market. Growers here for their home use have quit planting all other melons and plant the Georgia's Best, for it is the best. Seed white.

GEORGIA RATTLESNAKE, MT. SWEET, ICE

CREAM, THE GRAY, KOLB GEM.

We are just starting in the melon seed business—slowly, carefully, surely. Will send out none but seed grown by us. Have none for sale this year, but will **give away** to every one who will send for a small packet of **Georgia's Best** as a trial and an introducer of the merits of the melon seed offered by The Georgia Melon Seed Co.

B. W. STONE & CO., Proprietors.

Thomasville, Ga.

ALABAMA.

Tuscaloosa, Co., Ala., July 28, '94.
Messrs. B. W. Stone & Co.,
                    Thomasville, Ga.

Gentlemen: Trees bought of you last season were fully as good as represented in your catalogue and gave perfect satisfaction. They are now looking well. They came to hand promptly, and I like your system. I expect to buy more trees from you in the fall. Respectfully yours,
                    E. N. C. Snow.

Cherokee, Co., Ala., Aug. 6, '94.
B. W. Stone & Co.,

Dear Sirs: Trees bought of you last Februa.y have growed 4 feet. I like your way of doing business the best of any I have ever tried, I think your way, *no agents*, the best. Buyer gets agents commission. Your packing can not be beat.
            Yours respectfully,
                    A. L. Awbrey.

Pike, Co., Ala., July 26, '94.
B. W. Stone & Co.,
                    Thomasville, Ga.

Dear Sirs: The trees received from your nursery in the early spring were fully up to or *superior to representation*. Trees are looking fine, although having been planted late. I *lost none*. Your superior mode of packing and rapid dispatch delivered them in fine condition. I have never seen trees in more perfect order than the two lots I bought of you.
            Respectfully yours,
                    H. Foreman, M. D.

Conecuh, Co., Ala., Aug. 4, '94.
B. W. Stone & Co.,

Dear Sir: I did not find any fault of trees, *all are living* and doing well, and I just say I hartily indorse your plan of no agents.
            Yours truly,
                    A. G. Smith.

Roberts, Ala., Aug., 1, '94.
B. W. Stone & Co.,

Gentlemen: The trees bought of you last winter came all O. K. *exactly as represented* in catalogue. They gave perfect satisfaction and are doing fine now. They were nicely packed, and contained *extra trees* in each order and different varieties.

I think your system of no agents the very thing, for I can get trees from you for about one third what they would cost if bought of agents.
            Yours Respectfully,
                    S. L. McGowin.

Dallas Co, Ala., July 18, '93.
B. W. Stone & Co.,
                    Thomasville, Ga.

Dear Sirs: The fruit trees bought of you last spring, a year ago, out of 100 three year old pear trees I lost one. *Some* of them *have fine fruit on them this year*, which is more than I ever heard claimed for the Kieffer pear. I am highly pleased with your trees and the manner in which you ship them. Respectfully,
                    J. H. Rogers.

FLORIDA.

Florida State Horticultural Society,
Dudley W. Adams, President.
Orange Co., Fla., July 28, '94.
Messrs. B. W. Stone & Co.,
Thomasville, Ga.

I am in receipt of your favor of 24 and take pleasure in saying that the 500 pear trees received of you last winter were strictly first class (*the best I ever saw.*) They were nicely packed and over count. All are doing well.
Yours truly,
DUDLEY W. ADAMS.

Jackson, Co., Fla., Aug. 28, '94.
Messrs. B. W. Stone & Co.,
Thomasville, Ga.

Gentlemen: I am perfectly satisfied with the trees you sent me, and must say as yet they are looking very well indeed. Count, packing, etc., very good. Yes, we like your system of having no agents. My experience as a fruit grower, is very limited, only began planting trees about 10 years ago, most of them LeConte pears, since then planted some Kieffer pears, all of which are in bearing and doing very well.
Yours truly,
- DAVID EDREHI.

Alachua Co., Fla., Aug. 5, '93.
B. W. Stone & Co.,

Dear Sirs: The trees came promptly in good order and have done well. They were the *thriftiest lot of trees that ever came to this neighborhood*, you will certainly in future receive our orders. Respectfully,
A. LEYORAY.

Putnam, Co., Fla., Sept. 3, '94.
B. W. Stone & Co.,
Thomasville, Ga.

Gentlemen: Replying to your favor I am pleased to state that the trees had from you last season, prove every satisfaction, have made fine growth and are living advertisements, I assure you.
Yours respectfully,
JAS. R. NECK.

Alachua Co., Fla., Aug. 7, '93.
B. W. Stone & Co.,

Gentlemen: The trees bought of you last January were as represented in every particular. Out of the 1000 pear trees have lost but 10, but through no fault of the trees as they were in the finest condition when received. Thanks for the extras. Had more than enough to pay the freight. *Your system of no agents*, we think *saved us 25 per cent.* We expect to send you a good order this winter.
Respectfully yours,
CLARK & HILLOCK.

Jackson Co., Fla., July 25, '93.
B. W. Stone & Co.,

Gentlemen: The trees were well packed, some extras in every case and *shipped promptly.* You may look for an order from us the coming season. I say a good word for you whenever the chance offers.
Yours respectfully,
N. W. DEERING.

GEORGIA.

Milton Co., Ga., July 30, '94.
B. W. Stone & Co.,

Gentlemen: I am well pleased with trees bought of you last winter. Trees were very fine, well packed. Thanks for extra count. Some of the trees have grown over four feet in height. Respectfully,

JAMES JETT.

———

Screven Co.. Ga., Sept. 1, '94.
Messrs. B. W. Stone & Co.

Dear Sirs: The trees that I ordered of you last spring arrived here in good condition, being about 2 days, coming with about enough extra trees to pay freight. I like your way of no agents, allowing the purchaser to buy from the nursery. I do not hesitate to recommend you to all persons wanting trees, as you deal in only such trees as seem to be best adapted to our climate. I believe you to be consciencious and would not represent any trees that you thought would not be satisfactory to your customers, and when you saw that they did not come up to your calculation to discontinue them from your price list. Hope you much success in the future. I remain yours as ever,

WM. J. WATERS.

———

Montreal. Ga., July 27, '94.
Messrs. B. W. Stone & Co.,
Thomasville, Ga.

Gentlemen: I am well pleased with what I have now, and I am more pleased to say that every tree that I received from you has grown and done well. *Peaches have* done splendid, and attract the attention of all that see them. I am more than pleased, as my trees look far better than my neighbor who - paid nearly three times as much as I paid, and my trees take the lead now and I think they did in the start. *Every tree* that you sent me has done well up to date. And with best wi.hes to you and your business.

I remain yours truly,

WM. TUXWORTH,

———

Brunswick, Ga., Aug. 16, '94.
Messrs. B. W. Stone & Co.,
Thomasville, Ga.

Gents: I received your letter of July 24th, and have nothing to say as to the manner in which you conduct your business, simply this, it is purely upon busines principles, and must succeed. No agents.

Respectfully yours,

THOMAS W. LAMB.

———

Liberty Co., Ga., July 28, '94.
Messrs. B. W. Stone & Co.,
Thomasville, Ga.

Dear Sir: In regard to my dealing with you last season, I can safely say that you gave me entire satisfaction as to quality of trees and the promptness with which you do business.

Respectfully,

JAS. E. NORMAN.

LOUISIANA.

Glenmore La., Aug. 9, '94.
B. W. Stone & Co.,
Thomasville, Ga.

Dear Sirs: I purchased some of your fruit trees last season and am so well pleased that I thought I would inform you of my satisfaction. I found the trees to be all they were represented to be in your catalogue. My trees are in fine condition, haven't lost a one of them. They came packed in best of order, and a few more than ordered. I think your system, no agents, is an excellent plan. I find that your trees are better suited to this climate than any other variety. Wishing you success, I remain yours truly.

JAMES E. BLACKWELL.

Lincoln Co., La., July 28, '94.
B. W. Stone & Co.,
Thomasville, Ga.

Dear Sir: In reply to yours of the 24th inst., have to say: The pear and other trees received from you last fall were all as represented in the catalogue, and gave me entire perfect satisfaction, and out of the lot of about 215 trees, there are only about two trees which have not done well. The trees reached me in good condition, were nicely packed, and were in excess of the number I ordered and paid for. I think your system of having no agents is perfection itself, as it necessarily enables you to put the trees to the purchaser at a lower price. Yours truly,

E. M. GRAHAM.

St. Tammany Par., La., Aug. 13,'93.
B. W. Stone & Co.,
Thomasville, Ga.

Dear Sirs: The first lot of tree bought from you will be three years next January, *are grand trees* which cost me 10 cents a piece. I would not have one of them cut down for $5. The Kieffer and Bartlett were in full bloom last spring and have now a few pears on them. All my Japan plums bore, also have the Japan persimmons. Respectfully,

C. L. BECKER.

Iberia Co., La., July 24, '93.
B. W. Stone,

Dear Sir: Our order for the 200 pear trees of last year came to hand in good condition. They are growing nicely and giving *entire* SATISFACTION your promptness in delivering is admirable and we take pleasure in recommending you to the southern public. Yours truly,

E. A. PHARR.

Tangipahoe Par., La.
B. W. Stone & Co.,

Gents: My trees look well and are sprouting nicely. *You have gained a foothold* in this section and I shall recommend you to any I hear of needing trees, with many thanks for your promptness and liberality in filling order, and wishing you the success you deserve.

I remain,

DR. C. S. STEWART.

MISSISSIPPI.

Madison Station, Miss., Aug. 22,'94.

B. W. Stone & Co.,

Thomasville, Ga.

Dear Sirs: The trees you sent me last winter were *first class,* were nicely packed and on time. I have not lost one per cent of the whole lot of 1500, and have never seen as uniform and as full a lot of one season's growth since I have been planting and growing trees. Their bodies, which I always make short, will average nearly as large as an ordinary chair post with tops all that could be desired on such bodies. I would not buy Northern grown fruit stock when I can get Southern of the varieties I wish. I have *no use for fruit peddlers* and always buy directly from first hands. I expect to plant more peaches this coming winter.

Respectfully yours,

H. E. McKay.

Jackson Co., Miss., Aug. 26, '94.

B. W. Stone & Co.,

Thomasville, Ga.

Gentlemen: All the trees I have received from your orchards for the past four years have proved entirely satisfactory, and are as fine trees as I ever saw. My orders have always received prompt attention, and your packing is as good as can be. Your method of selling without agents is to be approved by every fruit grower.   Yours truly,

F. H. Lewis.

Clay Co., Miss., July 26, '94.

Messrs. B. W. Stone & Co.,

Thomasville, Ga.

Gents: You have pleased me in every particular with trees, they were fine, thrifty looking trees and well packed. I think your business should be known by every Southern fruit grower. Trees are looking fine now. You were prompt in shipping and liberal in count. I think your system is tip-top, doing away with agents. I prefer Southern grown stock to Northern grown. I have both, and must say that the Northern grown is not at all satisfactory.

Respectfully yours,

Wm. Schmitz, Jr.

Grace's Miss., Aug. 10, '94

B. W. Stone & Co.,

Thomasville, Ga.

Gents: Fruit trees ordered of you last season are doing very well. As to size and count they were beyond my expectation. I like your system better than the agents, system of selling trees. I believe those intending to plant fruit trees the coming season would do well by placing their order for fruit trees with the B. W. Stone & Co., Thomasville, Ga.

Respectfully yours,

J. W. Scott.

NORTH CAROLINA.

Yadkin Co., N. C., Aug. 21, '94·
Messrs. B. W. Stone & Co.,
Thomasville, Ga.

Dear Sirs: Pear trees bought of you last February arrived promptly in fine condition and were admired by every one that saw them. Could have sold every one of them at a profit in a few days if I would have done so. I like your manner of doing business and would advise all parties wanting anything in your line to order of you. Very respectfully,
D. I. REAVIS.

Anson Co., N. C., July 31, '93·
B. W. Stone & Co.,
Thomasville, Ga.

Sirs: The trees I ordered of you last winter came very promptly, only five or *six days from the time I sent the order* until the trees were on hand. Five or six years ago I set out Le-Conte and Kieffer pear trees and they are now loaded and some bending to the ground with fruit.
Yours respectfully,
C. C. BOWMAN.

Southern Pines, N. C., Aug. 1st, '94.
B. W. Stone & Co.,

The order I sent you last spring for pear and plum trees was promptly filled with fine rooted stocky trees and were well dug and packed. Everything was just as represented in your catalogue.
CHAS B. GRANT.

Edgecombe Co., N. C., Aug. 4, '94.
B. W. Stone & Co.,
Thomasville, Ga.

Dear Sir: You were as prompt as any man could desire. Your counting surpassed all other nurserymen I ever dealt with, and your packing showed care and pains. I think your system, (no agents) is a very good point, as you deal directly with purchasers leaving out the middle man. You care for the honor and high standing of your firm, therefore you will be duty bound to deal honestly and squarely with your customers.
Yours very truly,
D. B. BATTS.

Anson Co., N. C., Aug. 28, '94·
B. W. Stone & Co.,

The trees I bought of you last winter came promptly and was as well packed as any I ever seen. They were fresh and green and seemed to be in a thriving condition and in counting them I found nearly enough extra trees to pay the express on the package. I think your plan of no agents is a great saving to the fruit grower. I like the Southern grown stock as well or better than any I have bought from the North.
C. C. BOWMAN.

SOUTH CAROLINA.

Marion Co., S. C., July 30, '94·
Messrs. B. W. Stone &˙Co.,
Thomasville, Ga.

Dear Sirs: I am not only well pleased with my trees, your promptness etc., but I esteem it a privilege of which I am happy to say now, as I often have said to others who have seen the trees growing, that your prices, everything taken into consideration, was by far the cheapest I could get anywhere after having correspondence with several nurserymen and getting their reduced figures. Fruit tree agents in canvassing our neighborhood this season has not *troubled me at all.*

Yours, etc.,
N. A. McMILLAN.

Richland Co., S. C., July 27, '94·

Dear Sir: I take pleasure in writing you the trees came fully up to what the catalogue said. Gave full satisfaction. Every tree lived and are now growing well. I like your system. It gives me a tree at about ¼ to half the price as compared with other dealers.

Yours respectfully,
B. W. TAYLOR.

Spartanburgh Co., S. C., July 27, '94·

Gents: The shipment of trees and vines I received from you last spring were in fine condition, and were in all respects equal to my highest expectations. The trees, regardless of a very long and windy drouth during the entire spring and part of summer, are growing off well. I believe it is much better for us to order and set out everything in the fall. I have tried a great many varieties of pears, also of plums, throwing away both time and money by setting specimens, t at will not do any good with us. My experience and observations are that your selections are the kinds "we" can grow'successfully and enjoy. I never buy from agents, they feel no interest except in making sales. This fall I will order more.

Yours respectfully,
T. A. IRWIN.

Marion Co., S. C., July 27, '94.

Dear Sir: I was very much pleased with your trees, and have been preaching for you ever since I got them. I only lost one plum, and that was caused by excessive drouth. No agents the very thing. When in need of trees I will patronize you.

Yours truly,
J. P. DAVIS.

Marion Co., S. C., July 28, '94·

Sear Sir: The lot of trees bought of you last fall came all O. K., was on the road only three days. The trees were as good as you represented. Agents have been selling pear trees 3-4 feet high from 50 cents to $1.00 a piece in this section for several years, but I think they are about done selling at that price here. I have lost only one out of the lot.

Respectfully yours,
C. P. HAYS.

TEXAS.

Harris Co., Tex., Aug. 28, '94·

Your quick dispatch and good packing delivered trees in fine condition. I like your system of no agent, but you *could sell more trees if you used agents.* I think the Burbank plum can't be beat. Southern grown stock has proved far superior to Northern grown in this county.

Yours truly,

W. T. PAYNE.

Galveston Co., Tex., March 13, '93.

B. W. Stone & Co.,

Thomasville, Ga.

Dear Sirs: I received the Burbank Plum trees, they arrived in excellent condition, and they were sure *the finest trees I ever saw,* and I have planted them and will take the very best care of them. By the way, I have just finished planting out my orchard of 16,000 fruit trees; 10,500 pears, 3,200 peaches and 2,500 plums, I have the largest orchard in this part of the country.

Yours truly,

H. N. LOWRY.

Jasper Co., Tex., July 30, '94.

B. W. Stone & Co.,

Thomasville, Ga.

Gents: The trees were quite as good as represented in catalogue, gave perfect satisfaction and are thrifty now. They were delivered very promptly and were the most beautifully packed trees I have ever seen. They came during a very hard freeze, but were not injured and were as green and fresh as when they were first dug up. I, and others who saw my trees, are delighted with your system, no agents. The catalogues you sent me some time since went like hot cakes so that I have not one myself to refer to.

Very truly yours,

A. J. RIGSBY.

Newton Co., Tex., Aug. 27th, '94.

Messrs. B. W. Stone & Co.,

Thomasville, Ga.

The trees purchased of you last season were extra in every respect. Very large, well packed, count more than order called for. I think any wishing fruit trees should *give you a trial* and be convinced that you give perfect satisfaction.

Very truly,

J. M. HORGER.

Willis Tex., July 31, '94·

Messrs. B. W. Stone & Co.,

Thomasville, Ga.

Gents: The pears, persimmons and grapes purchased of you last February, was received in excellent condition, and better packed than any I ever saw shipped, and thank you for your promptness. I prefer your method of doing business to the agency system, I think. If you would advertise in the Houston Post Courier Enterprise and Willis Index. You would do a fine business.

Yours Respectfully,

J. D. MICKLE.

HOUSTON, TEX, July 29, '94.
Messrs. B. W. Stone & Co..

                    Thomasville, Ga.

    Gentlemen: The trees received by
myself and one or two of my friends
from you last spring, were the FINEST
NURSERY ROOTS I ever saw. The trees
and vines were better than represented in your catalogue and gave perfect
satisfaction. Evidently your system
of doing business entirely by mail
and WITHOUT AN AGENT is a saving to
the customer, and in the matter of
promptness is a marked success. Each
package received contained more plants
than bill called for and the package
was simply perfect. I THINK YOUR CAT-
ALOGUE VERY EXPLICIT, and that it
contains sufficient information to
assist a novice to properly PLANT AND
CULTIVATE FRUIT TREES and vines,

                    Yours very truly,

                            D. D. COOLEY.